HERE'S LOOKING AT YOU KID

	Page
Partings	30
Tristesse	31
Spring in Westminster	31
The Tower	32
A Harlequinade for the New Year	36
Bus Station — St. Ives	36

DEDICATION

To all spear carriers, one-liners,
Walk-on butlers and maids,
Third policeman, bell hops,
And general hoverers in the wings
Of the theatre of Life.
To second-row hoofers, high kickers,
The odd Valkyrie or Rhine Maiden,
Cygnets or attendants,
The seventh from the left
In the twelfth row of the Alleluia Chorus,
Ordinary Seaman JX 668 554
And Millicent Miller,
Even the fabled face-in-the-crowd,
And bit players everywhere
Under the illusion that History
Is what happens to other people,
When God or fate has already
Written the script,
And there are no second features.

THE MANTLE

(In Memory Florence Cotton 1898-1980)

The house, where my mother lived as a girl,
Was Victorian, for large families,
With small flights of stairs to be negotiated
When going from bedroom to bedroom on the same floor,
And at dusk, for light, the mantles were lit.
Small lace-like domes which glowed
As the gas murmured gently within them.
Their friendly white light
While not filling the bedroom
Did so sufficiently to reassure.
Pure white when new
The mantles would bake to yellows and browns,
Yet kept their form. One morning,
When on a chair to see the better,
I put out a finger to touch
And the dome collapsed
Into the finest of dusts.
A first lesson in vulnerability.
The latest, when burnt out by life,
She, too, fell into herself
At the long awaited touch.

KEP
(Horace Kephart author of 'Woodcraft' 1916)

Old now, he rests up alone
In the ease of mountains
Leafing his store of memories,
Advice and a deal of one-horse philosophy,
To recall the realities of the forest wilderness.
It's soft here in The Smoky Mountains,
Living no trouble if your needs are modest,
Hardly to one who turned survival into an art.
In rough times a man had to live
On berries and the hunting of bees.
For that you needed a pinch of flour,
Good legs and a smudge of punk wood.
The one for marking, the one for chasing,
The one for smoking them out.
Though *in extremis* you must starve
To know what you will eat.
Ground tree bark will eke out your flour,
While Sir John Franklin ate his shoes.

A man lost in the wilderness
Is a man insane,
Subject to the willijigs and the bugabee.
To avoid bumfuzzlement
Fire the ground to dry the earth
You are to sleep on and recover.
Where insects are vicious
Use a glaze of pine tar,
Castor oil and pennyroyal,
And don't go fooling with soap and water.

A good glaze is too valuable
To sacrifice to washing.
Sulphur dust in your drawers
Keeps off the chiggers.
For snakes and scorpions,
If you get bitten
A chew of tobacco on the outside,
A horn of whisky on the inside.
Both repeated frequently.
Use creosote for toothache.
For hysteria — do nothing.

To set a broken arm
Stand on a rock,
Strap your arm to a tree branch,
Then throw yourself off.
When you come round
Cut yourself free, splint the arm
And set out for help.
Charles F. Lumis did this,
And walked fifty-two miles
To the nearest habitation.

But solitude has its fine side
In a world where the four legged creature
That drinks silently is no dog,
And the woodsman keeps his pants on
'Cause they might get stole'.
There was a cleansing and a healing,
And the time of padded feet
When he dreamt by the fire,
And Titania,
The sweet queen, woke.

THE HOME DOCTOR

Its name in gilt on shiny red rexine,
It stood out amongst the 'Cyclopaedia's green
And the glossy brown of the collected Dickens
(Free with a subscription to 'John Bull')
This do-it-yourself of the healing arts,
This alphabet of ailments, aches,
And, more importantly, of parts,
Was my deep and furtive reading
From which I learnt the nomenclature of sex,
When I could snatch a time with it alone:
Nipple, vulva, uterus.
Until one day I met big breasted Joan
And soon discarded all the fuss
Of names, to share a wonder very close to love.

CHERNOBYL

At night the darkening maze of branches
Threatens as the forest broods.
They heard it fidget, breathe,
And tried to estimate its moods,
Read omens as the ghost-owl mothed
Its way across the woods.

Such simples ruled them, and the knowing
Pitied their superstitious pain.
Reason replacing ignorant darkness,
We should not see such fear again.
Instead, unlocked the nuclear void,
We dread the innocence of rain.

MATTHEW GOFFE

'And thither I will send you Matthew Goffe'

Lord Scales in *Henry VI Part 2*
(Act iv Scene v)

Words uttered, like the thrown stone,
Cannot be called back.
They and their echoes haunt
The caves of dark theatres
Where they settle like dust
Waiting to be revived
As Matthew Goffe waits
Faintly haunting his play.
You'll find him if you look
In the Dramatis Personae.
A name, like those on the memorial stones
Of the long abandoned dead,
Dispossessed and open
To the invention of characters,
Ready for development like vacant lots.
Hints are there: Matthew, bold, reliable,
A leader, he'll prop the citizens of Smithfield.
He is sent and dies in a brief wordlessness.
(Which is more than we know
Of the man who passes us in the street.)
It is as if Shakespeare was keeping him by
For a play that never came.
You need a character?
I'll send you Matthew Goffe.

ROQUEDOR LE HAUT : LANGUEDOC

There's a deal to be said
For a country that respects the past
Sufficiently to live with it
Rather than just preserve it.
So that, properly, it is a perspective
Of the present. Tradition helps of course.
Especially when you've only to neglect something
For a few months for it to merge in with the antique
As the sun bastes it and rust adds its largesse of reds,
And houses are patched not refurbished,
And doors are made out of old doors
Which themselves were made out of older doors,
And the ivy and morning glory strip the stucco from walls,
The heat stripping the ivy and morning glory in turn.
On the terrace each stone has its own
Independent level and invites
Weeds to establish themselves
Where the wild cherries are left as they fall
To make the air velvetly heady with fermentation
And provide a feast for drunken butterflies.
It is a world where decay is accorded its due respect
And the narrow road through the village
Is kept rough for the proper playing of boule.
That, as Thomas Hardy would have said, is history.

THE FILM

Clearing the house we found
Your old box camera,
Put away long before
You left for hospital,
And in it an exposed film.
A red roll on a black spool,
What could chemistry's kiss
Awaken from that chrysalis
Of time?

It unrolled to a back garden,
A son and daughter's visit,
A grandchild skipping on the grass,
And you sitting, content, in the last
Sunshine of your last Summer.
So close, so intimate,
So special as to be
Without point to others, yet
In its very ordinariness
Saying everything.

CASABLANCA

In spite of the box-office conventions:
The lyrics awash with sentiment —
'A sigh is still a sigh';
The hero reluctant,
Doing good despite his worse nature;
The heart rent heroine —
Husband or lover? one will have to go;
And the necessary soft-centred police chief,
Beyond these dollar-obligated fictions
There is a reality,
A fine feeling for the ephemeral.
'Here's looking at you kid'
The present is all we have
No matter how often we rerun the film,
So we know why that famous line
Is never spoken: 'Play it again Sam'.
Because he can't, because he can't,
Because he can't — never quite the same.

CLEARING THE HOUSE

We clear the house, empty draws of linen,
Cutlery, the litter of her life:
Old letters, photographs: In one a cousin,
In round spectacles and shapeless costume,
Paddles and stares out from her seven year
Innocence. Unfit for tragedy,
She was to be a latter day Ophelia
In a local river. In the larder
Tins for emergencies that never came.

His watch beside the bed. A last visit
To check, I stand alone in the house
Listening for the unheard echoes
Of a lifetime. I watch the curtains fading;
In the garden grass pushing up between
The paving. Motes, sun caught, speckle the air
As the house pauses with us before we
Continue without you, and time, like that dust
You could not abide, settles on you and yours.

THE SCRAP BOOK

He would not speak of it, or couldn't.
The Somme, the slaughter and dead friends
That haunted him for over sixty years,
And a shattered leg that would not be ignored.
Long after he refused
To watch a memorial programme on T.V.
When he died I found
A small neat scrap book of photographs,
Passes, medical certificates,
A cutting from a local newspaper
In which his name had to be searched for
In that long list of home-town missing
And the dead.
All pasted in just so,
It spoke to me. He wanted me to know.

FOLKLORE

'She's no better than she should be.'
My mother would say of Mrs Barton
Who with her frizzed blonde hair, lipstick,
high heels
And dresses she filled sufficiently to hint at what she had to offer,
Lived across the road with her dog and three grubby kids.
I found it puzzling.
What should she be?
And if she was no better than that
It sounded reasonable.
To be better than you should be?
It was a moot question as they say.
More than my eleven years could unravel.
'Then she's always washing herself' Mother would add,
'That tells you something.'
Well yes — but what exactly?
A reference to Pilate or Lady Macbeth?
Though they didn't impinge that much
On the ethos of North Harrow in the nineteen-thirties.
Best, then, to treat well scrubbed ladies
With an ambiguous caution.

SCHOOL STORIES

Monday

Sandra and Linda sit at the back for senior school assembly.
While the old man drones on about some hymn-writers
Called Herbert and Cowper who probably
Went round doing good to people.
They usually did.
Sandra, whose burgeoning charms
Prolong her evenings, dozes off.
She wakes to find he is still at it.
'Linda' she asks, 'Is it still Monday?'

Tuesday

Time to tighten-up on school uniform.
It's to do with reputation and encouraging the right
customers,
Or, more likely, discouraging the others.
So it is highly coloured and expensive.
'Girls at this school' announces the Head of Lower School
'Will wear school berets and nothing else.'
She endures a puzzled chagrin
At the small explosions around the hall.
The staff have to wait for the safety of the Common Room.

Wednesday

'Not bringing your P.E. kit is just the thin edge of the
iceberg,
You know what I mean?
How much, incidentally, of the iceberg is under the water?'
'Half?', 'Seven-eigths?', 'Three-quarters?', 'Two-thirds?'
The answers, each themselves a question, rattle in.
A silent panic — his mind's gone blank!
Why did I ask? — Have to say something!
'That's right, it depends on the iceberg.'

Thursday

The head deals with correspondence.
Dear Sir, we've got troubles again
So Tim will not be bringing any dinner money.
I've been without a man for two years now
So I hope you will understand and oblige.
Thanks in anticipation, Mrs Pilbeam.

Friday

A Public Occasion: Old Kemp is retiring.
Not before time,
The profession has whittled him down to a certain frailty.
Though it is surprising what qualities people acquire
When they are leaving.
'We will all miss him' says the Head,
'Especially the boys and girls,
He is the father of them all.'
Parents in the school hall look uneasily at each other.

Saturday Evening

You'd think I'd be free of the place!
The phone rings:
'Some youves is busting-up the bus shelter
Outside my house. I want you to come.'
'How do you know they are from the school?'
A desperate question.
'They're youves, aren't they?'
'All right Madam, I'll come over.
Where do you live?'
'You mind your own business,
I'm a respectable married woman!

TERMINAL

'Goodbye' they said
And shook him by the hand.
'We're sorry,
But we know you'll understand.'
The doctor stood there
In his starched white coat
Like an embarrassed engineer,
While nurses hovered near,
Their eyes all saying:
God! I wish he'd go —
Perhaps if we say something more.
'Of course, you ought to know
There are things we could do,
But they won't be pleasant
And our advice to you
Would be against it.'
'Thank you' he said,
Then wondered, once through the door,
What, in heaven, he had thanked them for!
For there it was, it seemed,
Most of his life suddenly in the past
And there wasn't much of that!
He hadn't dreamed
That it would be like this.
Where was the drama?
The cursing of a cruel God
Or a feckless and uncaring fate?
Or even the ineffectual sod
Of a doctor?
Not even a revelation!
But instead
A sort of numb sensation
As if he'd been hit on the head,
Or was not quite awake after a heavy night,
All greys, no black and white.
What was worse

He found it hard to feel strongly about it
As in the High Street
He watched the shoppers pass,
Their plastic bags abulge
With bread and meat and veg,
And reflected: What a farce!
They will still be here — still shopping
After — as if I hadn't been!
He would have shouted 'Lucky Buggers!'
But there didn't seem
Much they were lucky for.
A certain anti-climax
Overtook our friend.
This was not the expected end
Suggested by the films
Or on T.V.
Where rising music came before
The croaking of profound last words.
No hint at all that dying was a bore.

MARTIAL AT EARLS COURT SQUARE

1. Postious's poems are like himself:
   Too bloody serious by half,
   And doesn't he go on?
   He's the kind of man
   Who when you ask how he is
   Insists on telling you.

2. Amaryllis is superb between the sheets,
   All malleable bliss and eager with it.
   But then she insists
   On reading her poetry to you afterwards.
   An affirmation
   That there's no such thing as a free lunch.

3. How our Transatlantic friends
   Have a penchant for sheer length!
   The reading feels as if it's been going since
   breakfast,
   There's only half an hour before the pubs close,
   And they've turned off the heating in the hall,
   When our New World Chum announces,
   'For my penultimate poem I will read a shorter one
   About one hundred and seventeen ways
   Of making a pot of tea.'

4. Hermione, the generously busty,
   Went to the poetry reading.
   The oaf on the door remarked,
   'With a pair like that I ought to charge you double.'
   What did Hermione do?
   Hit him or kick him in the balls?
   No, she smiled, coughed up,
   And boasted about it afterwards.

5. Full marks to Nausicaa
   For discretion,
   When she announced
   That she would have quite liked to have been
   One of Robert Graves' Muses.

6. Gallus could charm a bird off a twig
   With his fruity mellifluous Wellingtonian tones.
   It is not until well after the reading
   That elderly maiden ladies
   Realize that they have been taking on board
   Poems about fellatio and incestuous buggery,
   And enjoying them.

7. Sylvanius's performances
   As an Old Testament Prophet
   Are becoming overbearingly convincing;
   But given his predilections
   Wouldn't Zeus be more in character?

8. To dine at Chez Cotton
   Is quite worth the bother of the journey:
   Good food, superb sauces,
   And the wine's not half bad.
   But as always, there's a price to pay:
   The conversation,
   And those terrible jokes!

JUGGLER

On reading a newspaper report about a man whose death revealed that he had been maintaining two wives and two families for some twenty years without them being aware of each other's existence.

How did he manage it? we ask,
Serving and sustaining two wives
And households all those years,
His parallel lives
Not converging until the end,
No one suspecting,
Not even a close friend!
Think of the problems!
Of Christmas say, or holidays,
The ingenuity —
Inventing different ways
To offset one wife against the other.
'Sorry dear
I'll be away for Christmas,
As I fear
My old Mum's sick again.
I'll have to visit,'
Or 'You and the kids
Will have to go on holiday alone.
I've got to go abroad. It's work,
I've just heard on the 'phone.'

What of the wives?
Did they complement each other? Contrast?
Satisfying different urges, predilections,
Giving his sex life vast
New dimensions?
Was one raven haired, raunchy,
Skinnily seething with surges of hot love?
The other pinkly silk-skinned, supple,
Burgeonly warm-breasted like a dove?

No. There was no contrast of erotogenic zones.
Far from it. Indeed, if anything,
They were more like clones.
Model suburban housewives, mothers,
Sharing a mutual ignorance of each other's
Existence, and it seems
Their drives and pleasures
As far from the erotic dreams
Of dark secretious love,
That jack up our own lives, as Pole from Pole.
Though even so
To have kept both satisfied
Suggests get up and go.

Yet that was not it.
As far as we can tell
The pleasure was intellectual,
Seeing just how well
He could maintain the balance,
A life-juggler who never dropped a ball,
Until he snuffed it,
When he dropped them all!
A cheater? Well —
He cheated us and God all right,
For he had three lives, when we have only one.
The third? So deeply secret and right out of sight:
The games inside his head.

DAWN

The mist layered in from the canal,
A dust-sheet the sun will pull
From the field's furniture.
Meanwhile, the streets are occupied
By a convocation of crows,
Black puritans stalking the streets,
Arms purposively behind their backs,
Eyes beady for the soft flesh
Of heresy, sharp pragmatists
Who will peck to the bones of any casuist.
Their creed admits no impediments,
They will clean the world for us
Until the town's business disperses them.

TORCHES

It is the torches I remember best.
Going home on a winter's evening
We would point them skyward,
Screwing the fronts to sharpen the pencils of light
That they might pierce the darkness the better.
Bold young challengers of stars
We competed in length and brightness.
Yes, better than the chips,
Tart with vinegar and salt grains,
In bags like small grease-proof hats,
Better even than the large orange bottles,
Tizer tasting of fruit that never was,
Were the torches,
Their beams like friendly knives
Making cuts in a darkness
Which oh so quickly healed
At the touch of a switch.

VENICE

Autumn is the season
For this watery republic,
When mists blur lines
And smudge colours to pastel.
We button coats
While the sounds
Of 'Smoke Gets In Your Eyes'
Drift across the Piazza San Marco
From the cafe quartets.
The evening lights switch on
Diffused by tide-glazed paving.
The concourse is on stage.
It could be Prospero's island,
The old magic faltering,
The air pervaded
By the scent of impermanence,
As this substantial pageant
Continues its slow, so slow,
Sinking into the sea that made us.

PLACES

Why is it we remember the sad lonely places?
Despondent hummocky fields,
Forlornly diregarded stretches of road,
Small dark arcane corners of forests,
Resignedly abandoned houses,
French villages on Sunday afternoons,
Seemingly deserted and only briefly encountered.
All possessed of a Hopper-like haunted loneliness,
The gentle dejection of places without people,
A fellow feeling
A sort of life after death.

KATHAKALI DANCES : COCHIN

The flat roof of a small crumbling tenement,
The warm air scored with damp decay,
A light pencilling of jasmine, a chalking of dusty cigarettes
(*Panama* 'Good to the last puff — the terminal fag!)

The performance starts
Against a backcloth of the city's buzz:
Dog barks, rusty crows, cries, traffic
And a confusion of rival roof-top dancers,
While remote stars quietly begin
To burn small holes in the velvet of the sky.

First the preparation:

A kohl-black landscaping of eyes.
Demonic deep-dredged greens for a God-King's complexion.
A saffron blush for his consort,
A top-heavy glitter of halo-crown.
A grotesquery of belled skirt,
And a long confused maze of explanation.

The cosmic courtship begins.
Feet and fingers and drums underscore
A galactic dalliance
As Gods seduce and tease
Towards a constelated coition
When the universe is consummated.

Still in tow from our transcendent encounter
We are asked for questions.
'We can explain philosophy, the universe, anything.'
It is late for such a generous offer:
An anxious 'Where is the nearest railway station?'
'Sorry, that we are not knowing.'

AN EMBRACE

A dove-soft breast brushing,
The ghost of a bird print on a window,
An exchange of breath,
A ministration of skin scents,
An osmosis of warmths,
A benign benediction,
A moment's resurrection,
A brief redemption.

PARTINGS

'Well buggeroffski then' he said,
Hoping the jokey expression
Would take the edge off the situation,
Would soften the blow.
She was indifferent,
She was going anyway.

She arrived at the station with her case,
To see the other he waiting,
Too clone like for comfort.
She hesitated, turned,
And buggeroffskied
For the freedom
Of what might have been.

TRISTESSE

'The thought of Heaven, however doubtful, helps to keep us going.

Warmly buttoned in her winter coat,
She appears to hesitate, to respond?
Between the fur hat and the coat's collar
Her petal cheeks are rouged and powdered
By the frost that hones the air.
Her fresh scent sharp,
And the small clouds of her breath
As sweet as mangoes.
Invulnerably vulnerable,
It is an illusion
She can conjure, quite innocently.
Can you lose what you never had?
She'll make you think so.
A razor slash of regret,
A fine gift, an image,
A fragile haunting.

SPRING IN WESTMINSTER

A thaw perhaps, days lengthen,
Birds dispute their territories,
Voices soften and the ice-iron's tension
And winter's stridency would seem to ease.

Clear skies and starlight seem exemplary,
But shifts in mood are like the rain
Where the easement is but temporary,
The style may change, and yet the thugs remain.

THE TOWER

The Tower thrusts squarely
Out of the mulch of history
Attempting to outreach itself,
A roof tempering its ambitions.
The remains of a long abandoned fortress,
Like an ancient surviving tooth
Decaying in the soft gums of the countryside,
Built to ward off attack, it sustains it.
In the echoing spaces of the Tower
With the bats and the pigeons
Is like living outside inside.
A paradox possibly more potent as a symbol
Than the Tower itself.

High above the small garden at the side of the Tower,
Hangs a great stone fireplace,
A massy reminder of a hearth once sacred to the
  hospitality
Of those named as friend.
Suspended above us
It is set in a wall that relies on gravity's crunch
And is patchworked by centuries
Of stone masons' botchings.
Lizards, frogs, snails, bees
And a handsome brown rat
Share the Tower and its garden
Where blackberries and vines tangle
And thicket in a vegetable profusion
Of banana and marguerites
That suggest a kind of tenacious survival,
Like the maze of myths and stories
We rehearse to preserve a kind of meaning.

Are there hauntings?
Perhaps
Accumulations of age,
A patina of ghosts,
Whispers of past presences,
Of the continuous present
Which is all we have,
Time telescoping into itself.
But that too suffers the sea-changes of the mind.

The mathematics of the Tower
Suggest even truth is mutable,
Which is the one truth we strive to avoid.
Will we never let the buttressing myths go?

The sun's warmth drenches the wall
Offering a benign drowsiness
That lulls concerns
As the pulses and the mind slow.
The lizards seek refuge in the fissures.
Thoughts drift —
A box of pictures from the past
From which the memory constructs
What might have been,
And myth overlays myth
To make life tolerable.

Then doubts trickle,
Soft flowing like the stream
That runs under the Tower.
The rat, a pragmatist, snoozes in a safe haven
To await the evening's foraging.

A HARLEQUINADE FOR THE NEW YEAR

The stage,
Our world, is set and so are we
To present Harlequinade
For all who wish to see.
And yes, you'll like it.
You have little choice.

Although,
You will protest
It is aggressive,
Sexist, that bladder and that stick
Not in good taste at all,
You can recognize a prick
And ball without much difficulty.

Yet go
To see old Punch,
Compared with him
We are a liberal bunch.
We just hold up
The mirror to your nature.

Isn't that
What theatre's all about?
And if we show the lighter side
And that's still rough,
You can push off
When you have had enough.

Though few
Do so, they have to stick it out.
'And there you go again,
More doubles ententes!' you shout.
But face it, we all know
For most of us there's nowhere else to go.

The masks
Of flesh or paint we have to wear
Cannot disguise our purpose
Or despair.
So while we caper and we prance
We do you service in the boils we lance.

'Told by
An idiot' you quote. That could be true,
Perhaps that's why
Our jokes are always blue:
But cut out the pretence
Your nature's such that they cause you offence.

Offence!
Offence my Columbine? Just look at you!
You weren't offended at the office do
When the Clown there slipped you one.
Why offence
Is retrospective, like experience.

What's that
Pantaloon, A red hot poker up your arse?
You're not complaining?
After all, we agreed life is a farce.
What's a bit of discomfort to show that we
Recognize Life's verities?
Come, where's your philosophy?

BUS STATION — ST IVES

This is a place of welcomes and goodbyes,
A level of tarmac that overlooks the bay.
Its world is on the move, small local buses
Or large expresses from the motorway.

The human exchange marks it a place
Of small dramas, hearts' meetings, fond farewells,
Against a background of a daily traffic,
A routine that casts its own peculiar spells.

That outlines lives, defines them
Perhaps, or even makes them meaningful.
Though there are magnetisms, so like the tides
They wax and wane to an external pull.

October and the shortening days soon fade.
At six the office closes, lights are dowsed.
Later the last bus drives away, the place deserted.
Can it be that other spirits are aroused,

Past travellers, lost, forlorn, abandoned?
A shade-like figure sits close by the wall,
Nibbles fast food and listens to the sea's
Soft sibilations that will outlast us all.

No stars, it's clouds tonight. Light sea mists rise
So it's uncertain shadows over there.
It's like the world's end and awake in bed
We're waiting for the last bus to nowhere.